LET THE WORLD HAVE YOU

Also by Mikko Harvey

Unstable Neighbourhood Rabbit

LET THE WORLD HAVE YOU
MIKKO HARVEY

ANANSI

Published in Canada in 2022 and the USA in 2022 by House of Anansi Press Inc.
www.houseofanansi.com

House of Anansi Press is committed to protecting our natural environment. This book is made of material from well-managed FSC®-certified forests, recycled materials, and other controlled sources.

House of Anansi Press is a Global Certified Accessible™ (GCA by Benetech) publisher. The ebook version of this book meets stringent accessibility standards and is available to readers with print disabilities.

28 27 26 25 24   3 4 5 6 7

Library and Archives Canada Cataloguing in Publication

Title: Let the world have you / Mikko Harvey.
Names: Harvey, Mikko, author.
Description: Poems
Identifiers: Canadiana (print) 20210375582 | Canadiana (ebook) 20210375604 | ISBN 9781487010690 (softcover) | ISBN 9781487010706 (EPUB)
Classification: LCC PS8615.A77387 L48 2022 | DDC C811/.6—dc23

Book design: Alysia Shewchuk

House of Anansi Press is grateful for the privilege to work on and create from the Traditional Territory of many Nations, including the Anishinabeg, the Wendat, and the Haudenosaunee, as well as the Treaty Lands of the Mississaugas of the Credit.

 Canada Council for the Arts   Conseil des Arts du Canada

 ONTARIO ARTS COUNCIL
CONSEIL DES ARTS DE L'ONTARIO
an Ontario government agency
un organisme du gouvernement de l'Ontario

With the participation of the Government of Canada
Avec la participation du gouvernement du Canada | Canada

We acknowledge for their financial support of our publishing program the Canada Council for the Arts, the Ontario Arts Council, and the Government of Canada.

Printed and bound in Canada

 FSC
www.fsc.org
MIX
Paper
FSC® C100212

CONTENTS

SPRING

I opened the car door and noticed
a sparrow sitting in the passenger seat.

Howdy, I said.

Howdy.

And I drove for eleven hours, through three states, attended the funeral, slept on
the couch, heard the whispers, ate the brunch, folded the sheet, hugged, hugged,

and opened the car door and noticed
a sparrow sitting in the passenger seat.

Howdy, I said.

Howdy.

WIND-RELATED RIPPLE IN THE WHEATFIELD

I love the shape of our apartment
as I walk through it in near-total darkness.
I love walking slowly through that darkness
with my arms out, trying not to bump
into furniture. How many apartments
have I done this in now? I loved
them all. Or possibly I just loved
how they held darkness, slivers of streetlight
sneaking into the fortress, amplified and lent
personality by the darkness surrounding them.
Wherever you are is a country. Touch it softly
to make it stand still. Your hair getting caught
in my mouth all the time, like a tiny piece
of you calling—like a tree trying to speak
to a rock by dropping a pinecone on it.
It is my intention to listen, but my hands
keep giggling while reminding me
I don't get to be a human being
for very long, as if this were the punchline to a joke
whose first half I missed. I arrived too late.
I typically arrive about three years too late.
I wish I had been able to sit in that white,
aromatic kitchen and look you in the face,
but I was not ready. I was still on my way.
I was lingering inside the perspective
of the spider I noticed crawling
along the baseboard. You fried
an egg. Is it possible to change

who we basically are? Thank you
for serving me cups of lemon tea
with honey in it. Even though
such copious amounts of liquid
would no doubt drown the insect
I imagined myself to be, that was kind
of you.

MICROSLEEP

A blue
worm works
its way across
the wall.
Electric
or natural?
I've noticed
the more you
interrupt
yourself
the more
destinies
you invite
in. *But then*
your own boat
gets smaller. God
visited — she
turned me into
a little flower
and gave me
this job: spy
on the pollen
as it falls
off me. *Does*
it seem
happy
to be
leaving?

TRAVELLING PHARMACY

Two women were jogging down Church Road when
a bear stepped out from the woods. They stopped, startled—
they had forgotten what you were supposed to do
in this scenario. Back away slowly? Yell? Make yourself
appear large? Instead, they froze. The bear approached.
He was carrying an old leather salesman's case. *Hello,*
he said. *I am a travelling pharmacy.* The women glanced
at each other. *May I tell you about a few tonics I have on offer?*
Meredith couldn't respond; it was already taking everything
inside of her to simply stand in place without screaming.
Bonnie, however, with an unexpected calm (a calm that,
recollected later, would disconcert Meredith even more
than the bear had), said *You may.* The bear opened his case.
Here we have a vitamin B blend that really helps fortify hair,
skin, and nails. It's one of my popular tonics. He handed
a small bottle to Bonnie, who shook it a bit, watching
the liquid bounce and regain its equilibrium. *Are you familiar*
with ashwagandha? the bear asked. *You take just half a dropper*
before bed, and it helps induce relaxation. I even use it myself.
Meredith was concerned that she may have some sort
of cardiac event if she didn't manage to slow her heart
rate down soon. Bonnie, meanwhile, explained that she
was already taking an evening supplement containing
ashwagandha. *Ah, very good,* said the bear, his facial
features softening. *And how is your digestion, if you don't*
mind my asking? he said. *Well,* Bonnie said, *not great.*
To be honest, it's an ongoing issue. The bear reached
a paw excitedly into his case. *Then I simply must*

recommend this ginger-based tonic. It settles the stomach like nothing else. The bear handed Bonnie another small bottle. *Organic, by the way,* he added, winking at the still-frozen Meredith. *Everything you see here is completely organic.*

FOR M

I don't
want you
to be
nervous. Maybe
thinking of
a walrus
would help.
Have you
seen the
video of
the penguin
accidentally stepping
on a
sleeping walrus?
It thought
it was
a rock.
The walrus
wakes up
like what
the fuck
and the
penguin scurries
off like
oh shit.
Sometimes it's
funny watching
a surprise

happen, and
not just
funny but
kind of
amazing — like,
you never
really know
what's what
when it
comes to
this planet.
Then again,
when it's
you getting
surprised, that's
different. Especially
for tender
ones like
us. What
are we
supposed to
do? It's
bad for
our hearts,
you know.
I hope
you won't
need pills
like I
do. I
think I

get so
scared because
I'm greedy—
I want
to hold
onto everything,
the world
wants to
take it
away. What
the fuck.
The number
of hours
we have
together is
actually not
so large.
Please linger
near the
door uncomfortably
instead of
just leaving.
Please forget
your scarf
in my
life and
come back
later for
it.

FUNNY BUSINESS

I wonder if later
I will forgive myself
for having denied my loved ones
demonstrations of my loving them.
I was too busy demonstrating
myself to the universe.
I was too busy turning
strangers into sites of worship.
I was so, so busy
considering the symbolism
of the fish's boiled eyeball
as it sat there on the platter.
I was feeling uncomfortable
in the presence of the wide
smile of the holographic customer
service associate.
I Googled what
delphiniums are.
I took my shirt off
and rolled around in the yard,
pretending to be a little worm
while actual worms were rolling
around in the yard and I
actually crushed one
to death.

UNEARTHING

At night sometimes
I go to the pond
which is a perfect circle
and as soon as I arrive
the gazelle is there too
standing directly
across the water
and as soon as I take
a step toward it
it takes a step away
and when I run
it echoes my run
and when I stop
it also stops
such that
the two of us never
get any closer
or further from
each other we
are just balanced
there two shapes
in starlight so
I don't run anymore
when I visit the pond
I just sit down
in the crisp grass
and if I wait
like that

for a while then
the gazelle messes
up its long legs and
sits down too
which is a fine
feeling being
at ease together never
having known each
other's fur

THE PROCESS REFUSED TO CEASE OR PERFECT ITSELF

Weaving washing oozing drying burning
cutting curving sawing drawing drilling slapping
snapping leaning bending rolling heating wrapping
sewing

    — the sea told me who I was, but I forgot.

    An eyelash, fiberglass, clay, rope?

    Ripping smoothing draping stitching peeling
charring bleaching hanging holding — so the sea
repeated herself, releasing into the branches

    my idea of what a branch was.

    Pinning pressing cracking gluing waiting
waiting — just
touch the thing
    & listen to what it wants

               to be kneading
beating dipping dyeing I
seem to be cruel without

    meaning to be. To be wholly fully
cool and complete, taming the pupil

    by untying the time
in which it is clothed.

THE INTELLIGENT ANIMAL

*I can't believe I squandered
those gemstones I used to have*, I
thought to myself, mournfully and
with some disdain, while at that
very instant continuing to squander
my current gemstones.

WET FUR

We like to describe the heart as heavy
when it's more like an old wolf
gone hungry, wondering
why bother restarting the hunt?
Then a rabbit emerges from a hole in the dirt
and everything forgives itself for just
continuing to exist. What's your moon
sign? What's your Myers-Briggs
personality type? Never mind, doesn't matter.
Or, okay—does matter, but matters less when we nap
side-by-side in this grass, the whole field
so American, all of our kings
somewhere else recovering
from microdermabrasion,
our personal wolves
playing around in the brook together under
our imprecise supervision.

HOW FRESH?

I had five juicy presidents in my palm, but decided to only eat two of them. Isn't it sad when it rains and all the little presidents wriggle up from the dirt, only to get crushed by our footsteps? My date had a piece of president in her teeth, but I didn't say anything, hoping the problem would solve itself. Presidents are tortured and murdered every day in exchange for their delicious meat. Presidents are shy — they tend to stay in the forest and rarely approach humans, which is frustrating because they are so cute! I feel bad whenever I kill a president, but it's better than getting an infestation later. It wasn't even about the bagel; it was about the lack of communication in our president. Sometimes when I feel stressed, I picture a baby president nesting in the hollow of a tree, and this helps me relax. I learned the hard way that you simply should not eat raw president in the American Midwest. When I told him I was finally ready, he was so nervous he couldn't get a president, so we just cuddled and fell asleep. I have this weird, recurring president where my high school math teacher calls me a *motherfudger* and pushes me off a cliff. In much the same way you can determine the age of a tree by studying the rings of its trunk, you can president the president if you look closely enough.

POSSIBLE CURE

on the inside
of your mind
there is a field
lush
and untouched
permanent
in its greenness
you can feel
it pushing
up against
your eyes
sometimes
so soft
it hurts
my life
one day
no longer felt
like my life
and so
I went
to that field
inside
myself
and pulled
one
just one
perfectly
green blade

of grass out
all I wanted
was a trinket
to help
me hold on
to myself
I carried it
in my pocket
but noticed
something strange
each time
I looked
the blade
was greener
it seemed
to be springing
forward
growing
fresher and
fresher until
it pulsed
with an alien
health
which
made me
nervous
because
well
I am almost
always nervous
so I brought

the blade
to my mother
who when
she saw
it said *Maryna*
there is
the person you show
the world
and the one
known only
to you you
can spend
a lifetime bending
them toward
each other
or and then
she fell
silent
which
was my cue
to leave
and leave
the blade
of grass
behind
for her
to eat

SOME SCHEDULED RELAXATION

To wake,
to stretch,
to breathe
and immediately climb
onto the trampoline
to become
the broken one, appearing
to yourself as the self
you have crafted
a life around
hiding from,
the humidifier spraying
its mist at a soothing
clip in the distance,
one feeling catching
a ride on the back
of another, arriving
late to the slumber
party I throw
in its honour.
Your Honour?
I must confess
my love for the ant
who walks in, then out
of the shadow
the trampoline casts: cleansing it.
Timothy
is his name,
but he also responds to
Professor Symmetrical.

THE FRONTIERSWOMEN

It turned out that the cause of her memory loss
was a family of microscopic women
who had burrowed into the frontal lobe of her brain,
hollowed out a tiny portion, and taken up residence there.
A CAT scan revealed this clearly.
Before she could really
process what she had just heard, the doctor
began narrating over a slideshow of images.
So, as you can see, there are four tiny people
living in the prefrontal cortex. Of the four, two
are particularly small; they seem to be children,
little girls. They pass the time
playing various physical games — tag and such.
The girls have two mother figures, one of whom
spends all day slicing bits of meat
off of the brain wall,
and when her hands are full
she calls over her daughters
who then eat the meat out of her hands.
The other mother seems to have more
of a maintenance or landscaping role.
And that's basically it. That's how they live,
hour after hour, as far as I can tell.

The patient was speechless.
But I'm getting ahead of myself, the doctor said.
You want to hear the prognosis. Of course.
Well, as you've noticed, there has been

21

some disruption to your working memory,
your mood, perhaps the structure of your sleep.
This is because, during their initial migration
into your brain, these tiny people,
these…frontierswomen, if you will,
traversed several neural pathways
and left a narrow band of reduced activity in their wake,
which you can see here, in this grey matter.
We'll certainly address those symptoms.
However, the doctor continued,
once again turning to gaze
upon the monochromatic images,
at this point the frontierswomen seem
to be going about their business rather sustainably.
The pace at which the mother is slicing meat
is so slow — the brain bits she is removing
so infinitesimal — that your symptoms
most likely will never get any worse.
Of course we'll monitor you,
carefully, to make sure of this.

A crow shrieked
loudly enough to penetrate
the window of the doctor's office, through which
sunshine was also silently penetrating.
The patient studied the doctor's face studying
the images. *Now, there is a surgical option,*
he said. *But surgery comes with significant risks.*
And, what's more, any manual intervention
would almost certainly result
in the death of the frontierswomen.

Which brings us to another point,
although I do hate to lay this
all on you at once, the doctor said,
staring straight into the patient's eyes now.
It is possible that these frontierswomen
are the only ones of their kind. If so,
certain scientific concerns, as well as
moral ones, I would argue, must be considered.

Or... or perhaps not. Perhaps
there are other frontierswomen, in other brains.
Living in brains all over the world.
That would be so awesome,
the doctor said, unable
to quite control himself.
It might even finally signal
the beginning of the revolution, he said, veering
wildly off course now, although
his voice remained calm
as ever.

DECLARATION

It's a fine time
to be shy! Oh, hello
to your brown eyes.
Would you rather
have the power
to fly or go
invisible?
Let's try
simply standing
super still, together
in high-resolution,
our minds polluted
yet still spry. Black
flies bite because
they love being
alive. Why?
Because thigh.
Dear fragment
of sky that stays
somehow nearby
always, remember
this: I am here
to be your fall
guy. Your battle
cry. Your basket
of wild blueberries.

MEAN BUTTERFLY

The butterfly buries its face in a purple flower,
and when a bee approaches, the butterfly slaps the bee away
with its large, stained glass-ish wings.
                              How best to commemorate
my role as witness of this moment? I could take a picture.
I could stare at the scene until it blurs to abstraction.
I could sit very still until the butterfly forgets me,
then grab it when it comes close. I could pull its wings off
and present them as gifts to the person I love.
I could do some sit-ups in the shade of the bush; the afternoon
is sunny. A garbage pile the size of Texas floats in a vortex
in the ocean near Hawaii, but that's old news. This butterfly
has a spotted torso — it's honestly stunning — and every leaf
in the park is making a slightly different argument
about sex, even the fallen ones, halfway to becoming dust —
especially them. I could learn the Latin name
of the creature before me. Almost instantly, I could gain a cursory sense
of its evolutionary history. The reason its wing
chose to be orange, etc.
                              There is not a single path forward
that's painless.

AUTUMN

93,651 guinea pigs
felt pain last year
during scientific experiments.
Noble pigs, we only wished
to know you! To know
ourselves through you,
and perhaps extract a tad
of profit from our knowledge
of you, and maybe in a few
isolated unfortunate instances
a smidge of pleasure too,
pre-approved for forgiveness
by the whiteness of our coats
and guided at times
by the light of our mission
to optimize beauty products
for safety and affordability,
so that even the children
among us, given
humble allowances,
could feel glamorous
and somehow televised
while gazing, for instance,
lovingly into the cages
that contain your brothers and sisters
(who are doing fine, by the way,
if a bit lonely, a bit gnawed on
by a constant, low-grade

uncertainty). I was at
the café the other day
with my friend Lexi
when she mentioned, offhand,
she wished she could be held
by a lover the way time
itself held her. What
would you make of that,
dear pigs, if you could think?
I myself didn't think to ask
because I was nervous and
over-caffeinated, but I think
she was referring
to gentleness, and possibly
acceptance, which are states
humans tend to crave,
believe it or not,
though we are not so good
at actually attaining them.
Then a particular noise
on her phone signalled
it was time to split
the bill and say
goodbye to each other.
As she walked away,
I took out the small notebook
containing my to-do list
and, with immense satisfaction,
crossed off *just do your best*
to be nice and not weird
for three hours.

FIELD TRIP

Calling all scared people!
We're going to pick chanterelles now.
Plus I wouldn't mind playing
some trivia along the way.
I felt so out of place
in the Gently Used
Women's Clothing Shop
on Court St., but then my separateness
became this nook I grew to love —
an old woman whistled
super faintly as she shuffled
through blouses, and the noise
trickled deep
into my brain, a kind of tonic.
I'd like to make that noise for somebody, just once.
Lately I've been hoarding wildness
in hopes of funding a rocket to grace.
I know, I know: it's not going to happen.
The only way to truly level up,
in terms of the Spirit,
is to start gardening.
My partner said several devastating
words to me in the taxi.
I stared at the haystacks.
I remembered my uncle.
He was the type of man
who'd maintain eye contact with you
even as he picked a live moth off the wall

and nibbled on its wings.
Lately I've been whispering
my secrets into jars. Things
can be pushed away
by inviting them closer —
we understand this, even
if the others don't.
Which is why I have always loved
the tiniest windows most.

MAKING A QUICHE WITH YOU

Day
owl out in
the middle of a windless

       wind, *discovering*
       a certain…optimism
       with its very fabric. When they must   *inherent*
                                             in the sap.

                                                 Kale: slightly

               wet. The first
  noise
       to leave —
  on the train

                           of your tongue

       — this morning
       your lips. And
       the students
        keep on
rehearsing.

FLY FLYING INTO A MIRROR

No wharfage, no
soft edges, no more
ice cubes or chances
to be normal, nothing
left of the landscape
that's photographable,
no imaginary friends
seated at the dining
room table
and certainly no soup there,
no fish in the river,
no miracles arriving
in the form of phone calls,
no signs warning children
of the dangers of falling
from windows,
no muscular sailors
who happen to be passing by
to catch the children as they fall,
no sailors at all,
no boats or water,
no gum wrappers left
to fold into smaller
and denser arrangements,
no faded bronze plaques
inscribed with history lessons,
no history, no ability
to silence the advertisements.

Are there some places
where love simply
doesn't grow as fast
as it decays? And by places
I mean people. And
when you fall
asleep is when
I need you
most desperately, because
without your eyes on it this
whole town disappears.

WORK LIFE

Happiness: the fiddle you don't have
to practice — which plays itself.
At least it's supposed to.
I don't know.
My job is to polish the jars
that hold the other, smaller jars.
My hands never quite relax, even after
I praise them for being good hands. Restlessness
is how they grieve the past, the dear past,
the deer that passed, then turned
and glanced back — I named him Tony.
The machine we have made is probably
unstoppable at this point.
All the more reason
we should not hurt its feelings.
Jawbone
on a steel floor, I am trying
to see you for the tree that you are. You make the room
seem smaller; I like that.
Nights blowing by like
the pages of a contract, so dry between my fingers.
We were picking blueberries, then the road ended.
We were tickling the planet, then the planet started
ending. Too polite
to scream, weirdly cognizant
of the meat I have eaten, I settle
for making intense eye contact
with the pharmacist.

On the last day, I think we will all take
a very long bike ride, and that
will be that. But where
are we supposed to put
the charming details we've been gathering?
The rules of games, the names of knots, the muscles
of animals subdivided
into convenient cubes
and exported by large
transpacific vessels, themselves
rather cuboid in construction, now
that you mention it: the geometry soothing
when viewed from a distance.

PERSONHOOD

This can't be my life, can it? Oh,
                    it can!
                    Sogginess
of canned peaches, I regret
96% of my backward glances,
but to regret is to glance backward,
and thus we proceed toward 97.
I regret ever learning about numbers
but at this point I can't un-see them:
98 steps separate the two ponds
— one blue, one brown — the two people
— one later, one now. Veronica,
it is said, works in the infectious
disease laboratory with Dr. Lucy.
She is as committed to the new
genome editing technology
as a sycamore leaf is
to becoming itself. One touch,
properly rendered, can cancel out
the previous touches.
                    Can it?
                    Well it
depends on the nature
of the touches, of course,
and the nature of the people,
who begin walking
toward each other now — 96, 94 —
the distance between them shrinking,

the distance between them curious
and nervous to find out
what will happen when it no longer exists.
Is there an afterlife for distances?
There is.
It's called personhood,
and it's just a variation
on the same dance you are already used to,
but hairier. A different heft and lurch
and lunch and love,
and the forgetting happens
much slower.

THE MOUTH OF THE DOCTOR

I went to see
a doctor
of sorts
because more
and more I felt
the bulking
of memories
inside me
and time
itself was crowding
my organs
and starting
to leak out
through my eyes
my hair follicles
my dreams
slicing me
at the sites
of departure
the doctor
listened as I
explained this
then opened
her mouth
to speak but what
came out instead
of words was this
very small owl

which had
been perched
on her tongue
apparently
then her eyes
went blank as if
she had left
the room although
she remained
and the owl
hovered before
my face
staring at me
with the same
expectant look
the doctor
had previously
been wearing
so unsure
what else to do
I began to explain
myself again
to the owl
this time
about what time
and memory seemed
to be doing
the leaking
the sites
of departure etc.
and when

I finished
the owl let
itself drift
down to the carpeted
floor where it
spread out
its wings
wide so each
feather was fully
exposed and in
that instant
a tiny
snail emerged
from the wings
it had
been camped between
the folds
of feathers
apparently
and like
the doctor
previously
the owl
now seemed
to leave
the room without
truly leaving but
the snail
the snail was most
definitely here
and was

in fact climbing
slowly up the leg
of my jeans
I did not
exactly want
to touch it or
it to touch me
and in
that instant
the instant I
acknowledged this
although I had
acknowledged it
only to myself
the snail began
to turn
around and crawl
back down
my jeans
then onto my shoe
then onto the beige
carpet and back
up the narrow
leg of the owl
embedding
itself once
again into the folds
of feathers and
the owl
having waited
patiently for this

to happen seemed
to reenter
the room
and turned
and flew
back into
the mouth
of the doctor which
had remained
open ever since
first opening
but it closed now
the instant the owl
flew into it

A MEETING OF LOYALISTS

Excuse me? he said. *I didn't realize I would have to carry my sins for so long. I was under the impression that someone would come by and, you know, take them off my hands?* I cleared my throat, eager to clarify. *Sir, you have to carry your sins for the rest of your life. Although it is true that when you speak words, create children, plant trees, etc., your sins do not automatically enter each new action* — but before I could finish my speech, i noticed that the man was only a mannequin. I was standing in the fluorescent light alone. *Sorry,* I said. *Didn't realize you had already ascended.*

SECRET CHANNEL

When you realize you are only a subplot
in the story the day is telling, you are
devastated; it would have been better
to be everything or else nothing,
but on your left front tire
the valve stem's cracked. She is running
downtown to buy a replacement
while you are in charge of covering
the leak with Scotch tape, to prevent
the air from bleeding out
completely. You drift from room
to room, not remembering where
you keep the Scotch tape. If only
you had taken a more thorough inventory
of your home prior to this moment,
this moment might have been avoided.
But your left front tire is bleeding air,
even now, while you chastise yourself.
If you don't find the Scotch tape soon
you will be sort of fucked, because
you live in the north, where the roads
are ice and snow. It's the sort of place
where mice find your apartment
desirable in the winter, worth risking
everything for. They embark on voyages
into your kitchen around 11 p.m.,
where occasionally you happen
to be standing motionless, silently

sifting through the minutiae of some
rhetorical stance. So motionless, in fact,
the mouse mistakes you for furniture.
You watch the mouse climb into your sink,
where it finds nothing, but when it climbs out
it sees you seeing it, and freezes.
The loudest sound in the room
is the wall clock's beating heart.
You and the mouse are both scared
in ways that are separate but connected
by the attention they pay to each other.
This attention forms a bridge, although
it is a fragile one no reasonable person
would dare walk across. It will collapse
the moment one of you turns away.

SUGAR WATER

(a pie made by hand)
(an idea about loneliness)
(a pattern in the dirt
made by a horse's steps)
(the accident that is
not accidental)
(the lake waves
resembling tiny
melting mountains)
(she asked, what did I
love more, structures
or her?)
(the hummingbird addicted
to the sugar water
we feed him)
(highway
raccoon carcass
up-close resembling
abstract artwork)
(the particular bitterness
of oversteeped
peppermint)
(what I thought
was love was just
a shade of purple paint)
(a scene from seven years ago
all covered in moss now)
(the sky reflected

in a knife
on a vinyl tablecloth
at a picnic)
(a child balancing
a basketball on her fingertip
then laughing
as it falls

DEPARTMENT OF THE INTERIOR

There is a footbridge
in a forest

almost no one
ever crosses.
                    The human mind is the moss

growing on its stonework.
I wish

I told
you the truth more.

THE BEST BREAD IN THE WORLD

The baker at the farmers' market handed me a loaf of what she called
the best bread in the world. Take a slice of this, she said,
spread some real butter on it, and thank me later.
What haunts me is the way she lowered her voice
as she arrived at the phrase *real butter*. No doubt she only meant *real*
in contrast to vegan substitutes, which as a baker she perhaps felt
were corrupting the very notion of butter. Still, how could she be so sure
I would be her comrade in this struggle? Perhaps it had something to do
with my face — some aspect that, when looked upon closely (as only bakers
and farmers and other such stewards of the earth can look) revealed a certain…
never mind. My arrogance is not relevant to this matter.
What is relevant is the feeling I get when I smear butter on this bread.
The butter, rather than the bread it was meant to complement,
has become the central event. By turning the key of a single word,
the baker reversed the ritual, introducing me to a kind
of conspiracy, and not the banal dairy agenda for which
I'd initially mistaken it, but rather the conspiracy lurking
underneath that conspiracy. The butter was real all along.
Its realness had simply been lost on me, lost in the forest
between experience and my face.

The next time I went to the market, I saw the baker, wearing her worn bandana,
and thought these thoughts, although I could not say them:
You were right about the real butter! And thank you, by the way,
for introducing me to the conspiracy underneath the conspiracy.
Such a crass statement would surely bar me, in her eyes, from the ranks of the real
to which she had previously assigned me. So I kept my mouth shut.
I bought more bread. I also bought eggs, radishes, kale, and a zucchini,

because I know how to play this game. I may not be a natural,
but with great effort I am nonetheless able
to move my game piece steadily across the board.

PERSONALITY

A tree

whose leaves

are tiny blue

windbreakers,

which, when they fall

in the Fall,

certain stylish

squirrels pick up

and wear.

AN ORDINARY WEAKNESS

The town needed a new mayor.
As usual, no one wanted to do it.
My severe anxiety makes me a poor candidate,
said one woman. *Oh please,* said a man.
That's nothing. I am literally a psychopath.
The meeting had reached an impasse.
So be it, announced the eldest librarian.
Bring out Harold. The glass cage
containing the small yellow lizard
was fetched from its official chamber.
The librarian removed the lid and turned
the cage onto its side, allowing Harold
to step into the light. The crowd fell silent
in the presence of a cousin consciousness.
For ten seconds, Harold stood motionless.
I glanced at Angelika, who was staring
fixedly at the lizard. The stakes were high
for her — I knew that — and her furrowed
brow betrayed it. I stared at Harold too,
directly into his dark, indecipherable eyes.
He pivoted, took one step to his left, then paused.
Would he pick Delmore, as had long
been speculated? A whole tense minute
passed like this, during which he seemed
to be gazing at all of us at once —
and not just at us, but also at our children,
our decisions, and all of the awful music
we had allowed to grow popular.

Without warning, Harold turned
and ran back into his cage!
We rejoiced, even as the librarian
began to weep. Of course we understood
what this meant: we were free now
to destroy ourselves in peace.

THE POEM GRACE INTERRUPTED

There once was a planet who was both
sick and beautiful. Chemicals rode through her
that she did not put there.
Animals drowned in her eyeballs
that she did not put there —
animals she could not warn
against falling in because
she was of them, not
separable from them.
Define sick, the atmosphere asked.
So she tried: she made
a whale on fire
somehow still
swimming and alive.
See? she said. *Like that,
kind of.* But the atmosphere did
not understand this, so the planet progressed in her argument.
She talked about the skin
that snakes shed, about satellites that circled her
like suitors forever yet never
said a word.
She talked about the shyness
of large things, how a blueberry dominates
the tongue that it dies on.
She talked and talked and
the atmosphere started nodding —
you could call this
a revolution, or just therapy.

Meanwhile the whale spent the rest of his
life burning (etc., etc., he sang a few songs).
When he finally died
his body, continuing
to burn steadily, drifted down
to the ocean floor.
And although the planet
had long since forgotten him — he was merely one
of her many examples — he became
a kind of god in the eyes
of the fish that saw him as he fell. Or
not a god exactly, but at least something
inexplicable. Something strange and worth
briefly turning your face toward.

HELLO INTERPRETER

Mostly, one
is busy buying
groceries
while the other floats
down invisible streams —
but, occasionally, the hidden self
can be coaxed into the functional
shell. What I touch
I touch then:
your earlobe
in my actual
hand. I open
my mouth and expect
miracles to fall out.
I look at your mouth
and think the shape
is miraculous —
possibly even
from another planet.
But no, it's from this one.
This one, where I spill
guacamole on a cashmere sweater.
Where I love
and obsess
and deceive,
and how real
your sadness feels
to me depends

on the quality
of the overhead lighting.
On who won the game.
On what we had
for breakfast
on this planet,
which I could not look
directly at while I was
on it.

WATERER

I'm not a man, he said.
I'm a deeply ironic houseplant.
And when I looked
closely, more
closely than I had
ever looked, I found this
to be true.
He was a houseplant.
What about our relationship?
I said.
But his leaves
just gleamed
in the flat
evening light.
*Can I at least
count on you
to protect my secrets?*
I said. *Things I told you
when I thought we were...
together?*
But his leaves
just gleamed
arrogantly.
*I can't believe
this is happening to me
again,* I thought
as I fetched
my little pair

of scissors
and began to snip
his leaves off—
cutting him up
just to be sure
he would never tell
anybody (this was before
even my little
scissors betrayed me).

SMALL GREY STONE

Worried Man is worried for reasonable reasons: he has been less than kind. Outside his window, a medium-sized animal is eating a small animal, while a large animal watches from behind the dumpster, biding its time. Worried Man understands he shouldn't be snacking on heart-shaped chocolates as if they were almonds. He is not a child anymore, which is worrisome. It is a simple fact that his mother's heart will cease to beat one day, and there will be subjects they never talked about. Such subjects blend into the mundane, like shy invertebrates eluding scientists. Such scientists return home to their husbands, haunted by the odd sense that what they were unable to find has now found them, and is watching. Worried Man's skin gets itchy — not your standard itch. His experience of the world is a grey stone he keeps on licking. Keep licking for as long as your tongue works, basically, is what all the books are about. He should have been kinder to the woman who made herself vulnerable by being kind to him. He was somewhat kind, but could have been kinder. The stone will be able to taste this on his tongue later. The punishment will be the usual: the woman disappears into the forest of the world, her absence a new ditch for Worried Man to pile worry into. When your tongue stops working, you are supposed to throw the stone into the sea. It is a small stone. Some people tuck it into their pocket instead.

PEOPLE NEED MOUNTAINS

Wall-mounted radical lemon cumlaugh — people need mountains.
Sense of place increasingly mouse window — the instrument revealed
less than it needed to. A teaspoon of pesto
should be sufficient to fill the belly button
of the househusband, but wait: we should reinvent gentleness,
all of the gates having shrunk overnight, leaving us trapped
inside of gardens we designed when we were children.
I can feel my fear breathing; can you? It's music.
Podiatrist-sniffing apology disguised as the alpine
layer — people need mountains. People need air
inside of their tongues. The lights are quite able
to take care of themselves, unlike the tiny bone
in your foot that is broken.
Do you want the dominant
mode to be regret or

tree stump for sure.
The smell of paper.
The accidentally perfect
shopping cart choreography
enacted by perfect strangers — followed by sobbing. This blizzard
we get lost in, does it love us back?
The cardinals are the carriers of the kink.
I am proud of you, still being able to fall
asleep naturally and all.
They will carry this away too when we're not watching.

SPARK

A leaf declining
to fall. A man
hunting to kill
but not to eat.
On the patio
last night,
a telephone
told stories
about democracy,
but I was watching
your hands move.
Picking up patterns.
Slowly starting to see
that my life was nothing
more than a perch from which
to be kind, like the foliage
that successfully hides
a turkey from a hunter.
The evening's blackness
frothed in the grass.
The evening's
mantises danced.
Or at least swayed.
Or at least existed.
And when I thought
that a small amount
of liquid was about
to spill over the edge

of your cup, a small
amount did!
Simplicity:
a doorknob.
The freckle
on your forearm.

OPERATOR

Does anybody
understand the body
quite like Becky,
the late-night
food truck
operator?
       I ordered you

a falafel sandwich

then later (a possum
motionless in the streetlight,
a missed call,
leafy silence)
we bit the backs
of each other's knees,

so hungry —

       the world
just a gumdrop
in a sea
of gasoline.

LIABILITY

Yes, people do trip over the wellhead
that protrudes from the sidewalk at the corner
of Pearl St. and Allston. I have watched it happen
with my own eyes many times through the café window,
a stack of reports piled up on the table before me.
What is the approximate age of the person who tripped?
Body type? Did they appear to suffer any injuries?
The answers may well shape the course of history
for Tidy Solutions Plumbing Inc., Mrs. Hart explained
while gripping my hand so hard it hurt. Yes,
people do trip over the wellhead, but the truth is
nearly all of them merely stumble then steady themselves
rather than falling down. Which is why it was strange
when a woman tripped and fell hard to the sidewalk
this morning. She remained on the concrete for a full minute
while passersby flowed around her. *She was something of*
an island in a stream... One man offered his hand to help,
but she refused it. I myself was tempted to rush
to her aid, except I am obligated not to. I am invisible
and, if anybody asks, unaffiliated with Tidy Solutions
Plumbing Inc. Her elegant black hat had fallen off in the fall.
When she finally rose, she did not appear to be injured —
was not even frowning, discernably — yet I could sense
pain emanating from her countenance, as if she wore
a face underneath her face, and that inner face
had shattered. When she walked away, she did so
without her hat, which remained on the sidewalk
for hours, getting kicked from time to time by those

who crossed its path without noticing. A young boy
tried to grab it, but his mother pulled him away.
Then a dog sniffed it, a good sniff too: nuanced, probing,
unhurried. The dogs' eyes closed in concentration.
From behind the café window, I watched this happen
and felt a measure of relief — knowing, at least,
the lonely hat had told its story to somebody.

IMMUNITY

The ladybug that landed
on your nose once
in fourth grade
and sat there for a minute, right at the tip,
is okay. The tic you do
with your nostrils sometimes
(when you flare them when you're nervous)
is okay. The fact that you skipped the party,
lied to your friends, and drank cup after cup
of tea alone in your bed
is okay. It's okay
that you never responded to Gregory's email.
Gregory is taking a shower right now.
You are nowhere near the mind of Gregory.
The evidence against you
is not damning. Even the little white
pills can be forgiven — they knew not
what they were doing.
But you, you know.
You get to watch your hands choose.
The ladybug thanks you for not crushing it;
the way this world gives thanks
is to fly away, into a tree
with thick foliage, out of sight,
where it dies and is born and dies and is born
on a continual loop —
what was the name of that song?
What was the name of that month

when you stopped loving yourself?
Temporarily?
What time is it? Has the boat left?
Yes, the boat's left.
The boat's going on a long, slow
trip up the river.
Then it's coming back.

LET THE WORLD HAVE YOU

1.

The pond wore a thin blanket
of ice. The ice reflected
the surrounding trees.
A goose flew
overhead and appeared
on the screen of the ice
briefly, passing like a taxi.
There were yellow *No
Trespassing* signs
and white *No Hunting* ones.
The signs fantasized
about the activities
they forbid.
The ice fantasized
about being shattered
suddenly by something
heavy, like a piano.
The goose guarded
her fantasy — which involved
a doorway, her mother,
and a pile of bones
— carefully.
I fantasized
about not having
any fantasies, and in
so doing drifted
even further from the pond

2.

because the young
people everywhere
wanted to be older,
the dinner party
wanted to be a raindrop, the sex
wanted to be a hug, the interior
to be the surface, the doorway wanted
to be a goose — it truly believed
it could be an excellent goose
if given the chance —
the tiny nervous
mouth sounds wanted
to be a symphony, the symptom
wanted to be the whole disease,
and at the end of the night
all the jokes that worked
secretly wondered
how it would feel
to be jokes
that did not.

3.

Knock knock.
Who's — help, please,
I'm trapped inside
a script I wrote
for myself.
I can hardly feel
anything underneath
these absurd robes
I put on
each morning,
so heavy they are
if not killing me exactly
at least harming the sacred
rabbit who lives
inside me —
No, I'm fine,
the rabbit calmly
takes a break
from cleaning
his paw to say.
Save your concern
for yourself. And
those you love,
of course.
Okay, well.
I mean, yeah,
the rabbit's doing
okay. Which is great.
But still.

4.

Still, if your life really
does turn out to be
a cycle of starting
fires, briefly
worshipping them
and then the next morning
sifting through the charred
remains for the most
eccentric little chunks
of wood burnt
black and shiny,
taking them home
and lining them up
on a shelf in your room —
I would like to take
this space to remind you
of the cat
in your grandmother's story,
the one who gets caught
in a bear trap, comes home
a week later with her hind
leg mangled, bone visible
and surrounding flesh
infected.

5.

This is rural
Finland, wartime,
no vets around to call.
So the family dog — generously,
or instinctively, I guess — starts to lick
the festering wound,
trying to clean it.
But days pass and
the leg won't heal.
So finally this dog, gentle
as a nurse, takes the whole tibia
in his teeth
and pulls it
clean off. *Probably saved
her life*, your grandmother
laughs, putting
her fork down.
And yes, we can all agree
he was a good dog. Good
dog, good dog, good dog

6.

but it's the cat
I want you
to remember
(does any other
animal address itself, much less
disregard the note
of affirmation
it insisted on pasting
to the refrigerator door
each morning in a rush
while reaching for filtered water?).
The cat who knew
she needed help,
and sat still
so the dog could do
the unimaginable.

When all the bear trap wanted
was to be the leg around which
it closed.

Acknowledgements

Thank you to the editors of the following publications, in which poems from this book have previously appeared: Academy of American Poets' Poem-A-Day, *Bennington Review, The Best American Nonrequired Reading 2019, Connotation Press, Foundry, Four Way Review, Guesthouse, Indiana Review, Maisonneuve, Missouri Review, Palette, Salt Hill, Sixth Finch.*

Thank you to the following residency programs, which provided generous support while I was working on this book: Catwalk, MacDowell, Virginia Center for the Creative Arts, Willapa Bay AiR, Yaddo.

Thank you to Jake Bauer and Kevin Connolly for helping me revise these poems and make this book.

Thank you to Andrew Battershill, Ashley Yang-Thompson, Christine Vines, David Hall, David Jeu, Doug Krefting, Edward Ryan, Florence Wallis, Gordon Harvey, Grace Sachi Troxell, Jonah Vorspan-Stein, Karen Jeu, Laura Krefting, Liisa Prehn, Maija Harvey, Martin Kessler, Nick Amphlett, Noam Mayer-Deutsch, Richmond Prehn, Riikka Melartin, Sarah Haven, Susanna Ryan, Sylvia Forges-Ryan, and Zani Showler — for helping me in all sorts of ways.